HONEST
Endings

A Social Worker's Life in the
World of Hospice

KATHERINE CULLEN, M.S.W.

Fulton Books, Inc.
Meadville, PA

Published by Fulton Books 2020

ISBN 978-1-64654-436-3 (paperback)
ISBN 978-1-64654-437-0 (digital)

Printed in the United States of America

To my wonderful, supportive and very patient husband, Ed,
without whom this book would never have been written.

Contents

Acknowledgments

I'd like to thank all my patients and families for allowing me into their lives. It takes incredible courage and strength to face one's own natural death. To the families who sat by the bedside for hours, holding the hand or wiping away a tear, I admire and applaud you.

The descriptions of people and situations in <u>Honest Endings</u> do not identify individuals. The principle of confidentiality is paramount in any professional helping relationship. Names and other identifying details have been carefully altered to protect the identity of clients, families and co-workers.

Prologue

In some ways, a hospice employee's work is never done.

It is not the kind of emotional grind one can easily leave at the office. For the first eight months that I worked as a licensed clinical social worker at a nonprofit hospice agency, I would come home in tears. Every night, I could not help but share my stressful, sad, often-traumatic day with Ed, my patient and understanding husband. It was truly an emotional whirlwind that only lasted three years, yet it changed me forever.

Hospice social work can be made all the worse—as it was in my case—when there are no systems in place for social workers to receive the support, guidance, or assistance they may need to do their job.

Helping a person and their family find their way through the morass of dying is a gut-wrenching journey and a unique experience each time. Relationships and emotions develop. When a client passes on, you don't just flick a switch, even though we were permitted one final goodbye to a family. This was very difficult for both the family and myself, having developed a deep relationship at times. There was no real closure. The bereavement team would take over at that point.

I do not want to call it an assembly line, but the transitions were jarring at best. As soon as one patient died, there was another dying client to tend to, another family to help plan and console. The new patient, not giving me time to process my own feelings of loss, would swallow up my own sense of loss.

Even after stepping back from hospice work, it was difficult to simply leave it all behind. A few years after I retired, I was talking with Ed, my husband, about that period, and—as I often had done before—I became very emotional and realized that I had never really processed any of my experiences. Lots of the stories still made me cry. And, in the parlance in my world of mental-health professionalism, that can mean only one thing: unfinished business. I decided it was time for this to change and began to journal about my experiences and feelings.

Working as a hospice social worker was extremely difficult, very taxing, and gut-wrenching, and there was never an opportunity for my coworkers to talk it through, partly because we were all so busy and also because there was no organized support system available. I have many feelings about my involvement in the hospice: bitterness, anger, resentment, sadness, guilt, failure, loss, and lack of completion. I also feel very privileged to have witnessed so many deaths, a very private and special time in our lives.

When I realized I still had so much to sort out, I started journaling. The more I wrote about my experiences, the more I thought that my life lessons could be useful to someone else—social workers, agencies, maybe families seeking to navigate the difficult path of death and dying.

In the process, perhaps, I could also finally put my own history with the hospice agency to rest.

The entirety of the experience changed me in profound ways. When I started, I was terrified of the dying process. By the time I left, I was completely comfortable handling dead bodies and consoling husbands, wives, mothers, fathers, brothers, sisters, and even young children. While I was shaken by the sadness, I reached the point of accepting death as a natural and potentially peaceful part of life. I had walked my way through many of my fears: What would a dead body look and feel like? Would I be able to put my own feelings of loss aside in order to be there for the family? Would I know what to say at the right time?

I also learned to take it in stride as my patients and their families discussed the physical nature of death, the need for living wills, and what funeral home to call.

Despite my own growth, this job did come at a cost to me personally, and I will share with you some of the struggles and the mistakes I made along the way.

My social worker's path to hospice had been a long and circuitous one, but I had always wanted to work in a people profession. I felt drawn to helping my fellow man in some way or another. Also, I liked the "social justice" aspect of social work.

Academically, I dabbled in sociology and philosophy, but I was more drawn to psychology. When I went to my first social-work class, I was twenty-five and I immediately knew this was going to be my field. It was so honest and very hands-on—a place where psychology, social work, family, and marriage converged.

After I earned my master's degree in social work at the University of Denver, I worked with pregnant teenagers for a couple of years at a family-crisis center. My job was to counsel scared young women who were not sure if they wanted to keep their babies. In many cases, those were extremely difficult decisions for them. There was a lot of high emotion and crisis management. This was my first introduction to real professional stress. My way of handling it was to share the difficult cases with my supervisor and to detach from the client's decision. During this period, my first marriage ended. More stress!

I tried my hand at a lot of other social work over the years. At one point, I ventured into more of a criminal-justice focus at a detention center for teenagers. I also worked at a safe house for a while and at a psychiatric hospital, where they gave me free reign to design and implement a program to provide counseling services to seniors in their homes or nursing homes. Another time, I helped indigent clients get the medication they desperately needed.

After receiving my credential as a licensed clinical social worker, I finally found my true calling as a psychotherapist. I worked in private practice for almost thirty-five years. That was a perfect fit for me. I knew I was good at it and that I could make a difference in people's lives. I was always a talented listener, and I knew how to ask the right questions, how to build rapport and trust, and how to help lead people to the answers they were seeking.

That is not to say it was always easy. After I saw a client who was physically abused in her marriage, I realized that I did not want to work with those kinds of problems. But I did have significant success with people who had suffered early childhood trauma, abuse, or neglect. I also did marital counseling, which would occasionally evolve into family counseling. I taught classes at a university while maintaining my private practice. It was a great time for me professionally.

In 2000, I began to have some health issues. I slowed my private practice way down. I always continued to have at least a few private clients, just to keep the door open and my skills sharp, but I discontinued agency work. My natural ease as a successful psychotherapist was wonderful, and it might have turned into an early retirement—except it was not to be.

Although I had expected to spend my fifties playing golf and quilting, the stock market took a big fall and my husband, who still works in the financial industry, was increasingly stressed and exhausted. It was clear that I needed to go back to work, but where? While I still had a few private clients, restarting a private practice from scratch is a lot of work in and of itself, and it takes a lot of time. Getting a job might be smarter.

As I was glancing through the newspaper one Sunday afternoon, I saw a want ad that would change my life forever. It seemed pretty straightforward:

> Hospice social worker. Provide counseling and social work services to patients with terminal illnesses, provide individuals and families with the psychosocial support needed to cope with death and dying services, including providing patient education and counseling support services for caregivers and families and making referrals for adjunct services.

I had never really considered working in a hospice agency before, but I thought, *I bet I could do that*. After all, I knew how to talk to people of all ages, with all kinds of problems. The position was for a counselor on a home-care team. I was going to give this a try. It never occurred to me that this might be a very difficult job, with many days of loss. I just forged ahead.

When I walked in for my first job interview, about twenty people were waiting for me in a conference room. It was quite intimidating. They were looking for somebody with experience in death and dying. I had done work with an older population, but none of my patients had died.

Not surprisingly, I was not their first choice. They were able to find somebody else with actual hospice experience. Still, the staff reassured me that they really liked me and thought I would work well on their team. Social worker positions are really hard to come by; so "luckily," I was still out of a job by the time the next position opened about two months later.

When I finally got that callback, I was ready to work—and more than ready to learn. I knew I had *a lot* to learn. But when I showed up for my first day, I was amazed that there was virtually no training.

There was a manual and a video, but that was basically it.

As it happened, I received the same cursory introduction to hospice care that the facility would provide to its unpaid lay volunteers. On day two, I was simply sent out with another social worker to observe for a couple of hours. Even as this "training" continued for the next few days, I was given my own caseload. There was not a lot of preparation, other than shadowing people and simultaneously learning on my feet for about a week.

Registered nurses with medical backgrounds, not clinical social workers, would be my supervisors as I trailed my coworkers into a maze of the turmoil, depression, and regret that often surround the end of life. What followed in the coming months was a nonstop roller coaster of emotion and personal and professional challenge. I have always been a very emotionally sensitive person, willingly to listen to the client's stories with great empathy and compassion. But this was different; this work was "live," not history. As the drama unfolded before my eyes, I found the need to push my own feelings aside in order to be there for the clients and their families.

I learned that I was very ready to talk to people—but I was not ready for death.

Chapter 1

Living with Death

Death is so mysterious, yet we rarely really talk about it in our culture. Death is an unknowable, mystical thing. Most of us deal with death as it comes, the same way we deal—or don't deal—with life. We either deny it's coming or fear the pain or the afterlife, questioning if there truly is one. Yet we all kind of go about our lives as if we are never going to die.

We often face the death of our parents as we get older, or the deaths of some of our friends, maybe the death of a sibling, hopefully not the death of a child, but everyone has to deal with death. Then when a person dies, the new normal happens and life goes on differently.

There are some "stages" most people go through when they are preparing to die. Up to three months before the end, people start withdrawing from the people around them. They generally eat less and sleep more. It seems they spend time in reflection and are less communicative with those around them. In the last two weeks, the dying can go through periods of disorientation or confusion, becoming agitated or anxious. Physically, their blood pressure lowers, their skin may become pale, they may sweat more, they become congested, their body feeling tired and heavy, not eating, but still drinking some. In the last few days or hours, the person may have a sudden surge of energy, which is confusing to the family. Their breathing becomes irregular, stopping and starting. They may be very still or restless.

Their pulse may be weak and hard to locate. They may have purplish feet or hands due to lack of circulation. And in the last minutes of life, the person will often be searching for air and, finally, cannot be awakened.

For me, death first came when I was about ten years old. I had a lot of fear of it; perhaps no one around me talked about it and because it was so impossible for me to understand. My great-uncle had died. I do not recall much about the funeral. But what I do remember is being at the cemetery and standing at the side of the casket while they lowered it down. I was terrified, confused, and overwhelmed with emotion. I prayed and sobbed until my favorite aunt put her arm around me. Expecting comfort, I was shocked and hurt when she seemed to scold me.

"We [the family] don't cry so much. You need to get control of yourself," she said.

That made me feel pretty lousy. It affected me for a long time, the idea that it was somehow babyish—or even wrong—to grieve over a death. I had forgotten about my uncle dying until recently when I started writing about my hospice experiences. This was another incident of loss that I had never fully grieved.

My next run-in with death could have been my own—at least, that is what the nurses in the hospital seemed to think. Around the same time of my great-uncle's death, I got really sick and no one knew what was wrong with me. They thought I might have polio, even though I'd had the vaccine, which had only been available for a couple of years. I had a high fever, a severe headache and I could not move the left side of my body.

It was very scary. I was kept in an isolated unit of the hospital. They would not let anyone, except my parents, come in to visit with me. Even then my parents had to wear gowns, masks, and gloves. I remember, late one night, I overheard the nurses talk about me down the hall—they said they thought I was going to die. I did not tell my parents when they next came to visit. I just stuffed my fear, and I began to develop an anxiety disorder that would follow me for years.

After pulling through that childhood scare, I had a lot of unease about death for years, but I never really talked to anyone about it. I have always been pretty careful about what I say in front of people, especially as a psychotherapist and a former hospice worker. It is difficult to imagine what those two nurses were thinking, even in the early 1960s.

My, how times have changed. I know I have. Today, in my midsixties, I am completely comfortable with death, and I am certainly not afraid of it—and not just because I saw it several times every week for three years. My experience at the hospice agency contributed to my spiritual growth, though ironically I probably would have been much better at my job had the two events been switched in chronology.

Years ago, I had been fearful of what it would be like to die, how painful and scary the process might be. Well, it definitely can be very painful. And it definitely can be very, very scary. But in hospice, we seek to minimize those things, just as many of us try to do in life. What I found is that, given the opportunity, most people want to delve into their experiences, both physical and emotional. I saw that as the primary purpose of my job.

In my experience, most people were either pretty calm or settled about death, or they were very anxious and unfinished about it, much as they probably were about life.

Given my then fear of death, I don't know why on earth I thought I should work for a hospice. It is not logical at all. But God clearly wanted me there. It was meaningful work. It is important work. Somebody has to do it. I needed a job, and I always liked a challenge. It turned out that I was very good at the job, even though it took a toll on me personally.

Sometimes I would have four or five patients die in one week. That was really astonishing, partly because it is such a busy time when somebody dies. There is a lot of activity surrounding death—attending to the family's emotional needs, calling the funeral home, assisting the funeral director in removing the body, helping to notify other significant people, etc. My job was to manage it all, and if I was close to the patient, I had my own loss issues to deal with.

Facing death takes courage of one kind or another. For some, the issue might be fear of what's next or the fear of being alone. For others, it could be the fear of pain, even the fear of embarrassment. For some, it might be a simple concern over what happens to the family dog. My job was to find out and to provide as much comfort as possible to the patient and the family. I never took it lightly. I did not just play board games with my patients—though sometimes that was okay too. (I remember dealing cards to one particular woman—she had dementia, but she sure could play bridge.)

Of course, in social work, you get used to separating yourself from the emotions. But hospice work was all so visceral that I could not do that very well. One time, I went to a patient's funeral, and boy, I cried hard. It was as if I were crying for a lot of other patients all at once.

One of the things I discovered about death itself was that it does not seem to change people as much as it brings out who they really are. My first client was Robbie, a young man who suffered from heart failure. It was a shock because, like many, I had always tacitly assumed that all of my hospice patients would be older.

I was particularly touched by Robbie's situation. I remember—he was so slight; he would sit down on his overstuffed couch with his Toto-like dog and almost disappear into the blankets. He was a veteran, about forty-two years old. When I first met him and saw his comparatively boyish face, my mind raced. What did the paperwork say? Was he really only forty-two? How did I miss that?

"Hi, Mr. Phillips. My name is Kathy. I'm your social worker from hospice," I said.

"Please call me Robbie," he replied. "Mr. Phillips is my dad, and he died twenty-five years ago."

Robbie's dog, a terrier rascal, came running up to me.

"This is Tony, and he already loves you, so you must be okay," Robbie said. "I'll probably love you too. Come on in. I need to sit down."

My heart melted as I walked into the crowded apartment filled with bulky furniture, blankets, and a comfy doggy bed. Robbie was all alone, except for his mom, who visited several times a week. He had fourteen medicine bottles on the couch next to him, mostly for pain, not treatment. I often saw this and finally got used to it. He said he did not like to take pills, that he had a fear of choking on them. Later, the nurse suggested he take them with applesauce rather than water, and this worked well.

The dying do not waste a lot of time on secrets. They tend to get right down to the crux of the matter. I respected and appreciated Robbie's candor. I am that way myself. Robbie would chat away. One day he shared that he was still a virgin. That was very difficult for him to talk about. He was shy and insecure and had not had any long-term relationships. He had wanted sex to be important, and he had never really fallen in love.

On the other hand, Robbie was very accepting of his fatal condition. His father and uncle had both died of heart disease at an early age, and he had outlived both of them.

Robbie's mother was not overly emotional, at least not while I was around—until the day they had to take him to the Veterans Administration Hospital in Denver. I had just happened to stop by that day, and I was shocked to see him being loaded into an ambulance. He simply could not make it up those apartment stairs anymore.

Mom was there, teary-eyed. Tony, the dog, was racing around all over the place.

Robbie seemed glad to be finally going to the VA. He would not have to do it all by himself anymore. He grabbed my hand from the gurney and thanked me as tears welled up in his eyes.

"I'll never forget you, your attitude toward me," he said. "You always treated me like a person, not a patient, with respect and caring. You are special. Now, go home and take care of Kathy, will you?"

My eyes were wet by this time. I quietly hugged him. I was so grateful that I would not have to watch this young man die.

I would not be so fortunate with Esther, one of my toughest clients.

It had been a long road for this very sad woman. She was fifty-nine and had breast cancer, which had, by this point, spread to her liver. At first, Esther did not want anything to do with hospice care, even though her doctor had recommended it. Instead, she desperately wanted the doctors to keep treating her. She was convinced that they had not done a good-enough job. She was very critical about a lot of other things too.

Esther had a very difficult time with relationships, usually keeping people at arm's length. Apparently, she had been that way her entire life, according to what I heard from her family. I viewed her troubled state of mind as a challenge and wanted to have a relationship with her anyway. We did not talk much about death. We discussed other things—like how bad life was.

As a confirmed atheist, there was not even a sense of peace in death for Esther. She had this terrible fear of what was to come next—but she didn't have a faith to call on, so there was no answer for it, other than us just going away. She was a challenging woman to have a relationship with, but she really wanted me to visit. And so I went. After a while, we got along.

Unfortunately, Esther had a horrible relationship with her father, a kind and well-meaning man, who was an Evangelical Christian. One day he came to his daughter's room, not to console her or say goodbye, but to shout and scream, "You're going to hell!" The father's minister even tried to do an on-the-spot conversion. That did not go well. Esther wanted no part of any organized religion—or any religion, period. I did not have much spiritual belief myself at that time, but it was hard for me that she had nothing at all.

At one point, Esther could not even walk from her living room to the kitchen more than once a day. So by the end, she wound up in a nursing home, which she hated. This was my first death in a nursing home—facilities that I had never liked to begin with. The smell was dreadful. The sounds were loud and often full of anguish.

By the time Esther died, her older sister, Susan, was in town. The two were very close in a certain way. It was very hard for Susan to lose her baby sister.

As Esther lay dying, she did not seem restless, which can be a sign of anxiety, but she had a very tense facial expression. I asked the nurse on the floor if she could give her something for anxiety, and she did. Esther had expressed a great fear of pain. After the medication was given, her face relaxed and her breathing became slower.

I encouraged Susan to come closer to talk to her sister, to hold her hand if she wanted to. I told her it would not be too much longer.

"She knows you're here, and it is comforting to her," I said.

Susan held Esther's hand and said goodbye, crying. She told her sister that she loved her and said she was sorry that her life had been so hard.

Esther would soon take her last breath, with a shudder, startling both of us, but it was a fairly peaceful passing. I suddenly became very emotional inside. I looked at Susan, who also had tears in her eyes. We just stood by her body for a few minutes. We cried together.

I soon explained that the bereavement team would be calling. Again, an unwelcome surprise to Susan—she had assumed that she could do her grief work with me.

Chapter 2

Welcome Aboard

Hospice agencies are designed to help terminal patients through the last six months or so of their lives. Insurance and Medicare have basically created that formula. Some people would be in our hospice for a few hours, literally. Some would be with us for a week or less. Less often, we would care for a patient for several months, particularly those with heart disease or dementia.

There is a lot of denial and resistance to getting this kind of help at the end of life. Sometimes there was not even time to make one visit.

This was quite a change for me. Because my background was in psychotherapy, I was used to fairly intimate, longer-term relationships with time to build rapport and trust. In hospice, we often had to build trust very quickly and delve into a person's most intimate issues right away.

There are two basic components to hospice care.

A hospice nurse helps patients manage their symptoms, as well as their pain and anxiety medications. The nurse would also take patients' vital signs and answer whatever medical questions they had as they approached their final months, weeks, or days. Some who come into hospice have already been prescribed antidepressants, which would be continued. Nurses are generally trained to come into a situation, fix it, and leave. Social workers are trained in process; we could take time to get to know the dying person as well as the family and friends and help everyone express their concerns and desires.

A social worker would do an emotional and social family assessment. We would consider all the aspects of a person's life, the support systems they may or may not have, and their emotional needs. We would also help facilitate the legal aspects, paperwork, wills, power of attorney, and final directives. Just getting that done is a lot of comfort to hospice patients.

Of course, we also had some very officious things to do like filling out intake forms and broaching some awkward questions. I would have to find out which funeral home the family or patient wanted us to call when the time came. That was a difficult one for me at first, but there were others. Do you even want a funeral? What kind of a service do you want? Do you want to be cremated or buried?

Sometimes the patients did not have any idea how to answer. When you pick a funeral home, that is pretty much cutting through the denial. Everything becomes very real. When life and death get emotional, it can be easy to overlook administrative detail.

There was one case where I forgot to get the paperwork to assign a patient's son as the power of attorney. I had to hustle to get it done in time. He was a Hispanic man whose family was very traditional. It was so important to him to pass everything on to his son before he died, and I had waited nearly too long.

Beyond such tasks, everything that I did was to support the patient in one way or another. Even just showing up and spending a few minutes talking with them or their family could be extremely important. In our hospice, there were six social workers on two teams.

When it comes down to it, hospice care is mostly about quality of life and easing pain, discomfort, and anxiety in a person's final days or hours. I went out on a call with a supervising nurse. I remember feeling nervous because she was there to evaluate my work. The man we visited suffered from pancreatic cancer. He had pain, but what really drove him crazy were his nonstop hiccups. He could barely sleep for several days. The nurse with me knew of a prescription medication for that. Who knew? I didn't. I made a call to the on-call RN and asked if she could get a doctor's order for this medication. She agreed, and we left shortly after. Kate, the supervisor, paid me a compliment as she said, "I know which social worker I'd want on my

case if I were a patient. You're very empathetic and compassionate."
Wow—that felt amazing!

Beyond the RN and the social worker, we had music thera-
pists who would provide a very different sort of emotional support.
We had chaplains who would address the spiritual needs if patients
wanted that support. We could provide volunteers for everything
from providing rides to appointments to sitting vigil with the dying
patient while the family took a much-needed break. All these services
were optional, including the social worker—everything except the
nurse, which is the only requirement of hospice care.

To clarify, "going" to hospice is not literal, at least not at our
agency. Hospice was not a place in our town. Our patients were living in traditional homes, assisted-living facilities, or nursing homes,
though one local hospital had an small inpatient hospice unit where
we would provide our services. Having said that, if a patient happens
to be in a hospital for some reason, he or she cannot receive the
hospice's services, which might sound sort of weird, but that's the
way it is. It has to be one or the other. There is a difference between
palliative care (hospice) and treatment (hospital).

As a social worker, by the way, I was accustomed to calling people "clients." But this was a medical model, designed by doctors and
run by nurses, so we called them "patients."

In any case, these "patients" were generally not going to get
"better," and that was part of the bargain. The medications adminis-
tered were for pain, anxiety, and depression, not to treat the person's
fatal condition. Sometimes patients would still be given high-blood-
pressure medicine, but no more chemotherapy. This was purely comfort care.

Similarly, our patients also had to sign a do-not-resuscitate (or
DNR) order. It was required. You could not be a hospice patient if
you still wanted to be resuscitated.

One of my first on-duty deaths was a woman in her eighties.
Her daughter, Amy, had not yet signed the DNR order, and she was
reluctant to sign it now, unsure of her mother's wishes. We were supposed to get the DNR signed at intake, but somehow it had been
missed this time.

I tried to explain to Amy that if the DNR was not signed and her mom's heart stops, we would have to call 911. They would come and try to bring her back, and that can be a painful process. Amy was in a very tough position. Either she signs it right now or we call 911. She had just minutes to decide.

She signed it. Her mom died right away.

Amy collapsed on her mother's chest and immediately began to wonder if she had done the right thing. I reassured her that her mom would not have agreed to hospice services if she was not ready to go. I wonder about Amy sometimes. I hope she eventually accepted her decision.

Incidentally, I had one patient who actually survived the hospice. She was a Russian woman who had gotten breast cancer as a result of the Chernobyl disaster of the 1980s. But she got better. Everyone was ecstatic when her scans had come back negative. She was discharged. That was a good day.

A difficult adjustment for me was the concept of a "good death." Of course, that meant different things to different people. Do you want your loved ones around you? Do you want to be at home, or do you want to be in a facility of some kind?

The big one: what's most important—pain control or being alert? You could not have both. Death can be painful. A dying body is slowly giving up its grasp. The fact is, if you treat the pain, you are going to be less alert to your surroundings. People have to decide. It can be a very difficult choice.

The two things that seemed to interfere most with a peaceful death were fear and pain. The nurse could almost always handle the pain with appropriate medications. The social worker, on the other hand, addressed the fears and other emotions, helped the family voice their concerns and feelings. What could we do to make death less scary? That varied from person to person. Sometimes it was a fear of being alone. Often it was the fear of what's coming next. Sometimes this called for a chaplain. Other times, the patient wanted to talk with me.

As I mentioned, I started seeing my own clients—or patients—on the very week I went on payroll. This was, of course, crazy, at least from my standpoint. I could have used some verbal instructions or advice about what to expect, perhaps even some role-playing of patient scenarios. I had been used to working with people who would talk about things that had already happened in their lives, their history or a difficult situation. But now my clients were not just talking about it—they were living it. It was right there in front of me.

I would arrive at a home and find a fight already going on. Instead of hearing about the domestic conflict, I would be seeing it. It was like live-action psychotherapy.

I probably saw three or four patients on that first day. All were unique situations. I never knew exactly what I was going to discover. The intake team would go out first, meet the patient, qualify them for hospice, and then give a report about that person on the phone, which was mostly medical.

Robbie, my first patient, the younger veteran, had made the choice to be pain-free. As a result, he became more confused, and that added to his inability to take care of himself. Eventually, it was time to ask once again, "Are you still comfortable with this choice?" He was.

As it turned out, most people selected pain control, but not all. I had one patient who, like Robbie, was on the younger side. She had breast cancer that had metastasized, and she did not want to give up her mental acuity. She really wanted to know what was going on. She suffered a lot of pain as a result, but she wanted to stay alert until the very end. My job was to support her decision.

It really comes down to a matter of "picking one's poison." But sometimes we would find other ways to lessen the pain. We could find a volunteer to "distract" a patient—with a massage or a nail treatment or by reading to them. Things like that could enhance a person's life and divert them from their discomfort for a while.

But there were times when the pain was not the kind that was treatable with painkillers or distractions. I got very close to some patients who would share their most closely held secrets with me. Hospice patients tended to get very honest very quickly. There is no bullshitting when you are dying. You get right down to it.

As a therapist, most people would eventually talk to me about things they had never told anyone else. But in hospice, many patients would very quickly let down whatever barriers they had. One man confessed incest. Another woman had lived a secret life as a lesbian, only telling me near the very end of her life. Many people felt it was finally time to talk. What was left to lose? I valued their courage and trust.

Many times I was there when my patients died, though it was amazing how many people were alone at the moment they passed away. In nursing homes, families would sit vigil and then step out for a five-minute break. The person would die before they got back. It is almost as though some people want to be alone when they go. Others would wait for a loved one to arrive and then die quietly.

I remember the first time a funeral director wanted me to help move a body onto the gurney. He just kind of walked me through the process in a very respectful way; gently rolling the person's body inside a sheet then carefully onto the gurney and rolling it carefully to the waiting vehicle. This was certainly a stretch of my comfort zone. But after a while, I got used to that, and it did feel like I was doing a final service for the person.

Unfortunately, there was little to no time for "processing" it all among ourselves as social workers. We would "officially" share our cases in rapid-fire meetings every other week—thirty cases in ninety minutes, superficially, one right after the other. These meetings were largely focused on the physical symptoms of the patient with very little time given to the emotional or spiritual. I was seeing twenty to twenty-five patients or more a week and working forty to fifty hours every week when I was full-time.

On top of the daily stress, we could even occasionally find ourselves in potentially dangerous situations. Early on, I got a middle-of-the-night phone call of an impending death and was told that drugs or alcohol might be present. The on-duty nurse who called did not want to go with me. I thought we should go together, but I did not feel comfortable saying so at the time. I just figured I would call the police if need be. As it turned out, everything was fine—just more family dynamics.

Suffice it to say that this agency was not a place for much professional support, peer discussion, or helpful consultation. I might see four or five people in a day, many of them in the midst of emotionally heightened situations. I would then go home without having discussed my cases with anyone at work. Instead, I would just share it all with Ed, my husband. He really wanted to be there for me and always has been, but I am sure he got tired of it.

The next day, it would start all over again.

In between those shifts, I cried many times. I do not think this is typical for new caseworkers, but I am definitely a crier. I had to go through my own process of getting used to death and dying. My daily life was this constant pushing of it all aside, focusing on whatever task was right in front of me, and doing the best I could with it. Still, everybody received good care—except perhaps the employees.

I have no idea what my supervisors were thinking, but no one ever asked me any questions about my cases. What does that say? "Don't talk about it." So that is exactly what I decided to do, and that was not a good idea. I had to either process with Ed or just stuff my feelings. Ed is great at listening, but he didn't know what to do. He is a finance guy. He would just be there for me, for which I am very, very grateful.

When I was first hired, a social worker was the Team Leader. But within two weeks, the structure changed, and an RN took that position. This was a difficult change for me, as I felt I had no one in my field available for consultation. A couple of times I tried going to the RN, my supervisor, to get counsel on difficult cases, but she was not helpful.

At least, she admitted it.

"Look, you know, I'm an RN. I don't really know what it is you do or how to help you," she said.

That conversation sprang from a case of a woman in her early 40's with lung cancer. She had three kids, one of them very young, and a husband who was very busy with work and providing for the family financially, but not very available otherwise. Their niece was caring for the children, and she was feeling overwhelmed and wanted her uncle to be more involved emotionally.

My supervisor's expertise was in medication and symptom management, not family dynamics.

"Talk to Ruth about it," the nurse suggested.

Ruth was a social worker who had been there a long time. She was just as busy and just as unsupported as I was. I could have gone to her for her thoughts, but it would have been a lengthy conversation, too complicated for the watercooler. So I didn't go to Ruth. I just kind of winged it.

The next day, I talked with the niece and suggested she support the heck out of those kids. I said a lot of times husbands pull away because they are in too much pain themselves. The niece had never thought of it that way. She had thought about her own pain, believing the husband was just being mean in not attending to his sickly wife. I tried to reframe that a little bit for her, and it seemed to help.

Like the RN, the hospice's new executive director was not particularly helpful. Frankly, he did not know what he was doing at all. He had been promoted from his previous position as assistant director. This was against the recommendation of the staff, but the board hired him anyway. He took a dislike to me immediately. I was outspoken in meetings and had ideas about how things could be better.

Admittedly, I had been in private practice for twenty years, running my own show. I was not used to having a boss, much less one that did not have a clear understanding of what I did. In all my time on the job, the director never once came over to talk to any of us about our daily responsibilities. He was not a nurse or a social worker. It was always unclear what qualifications he even had.

When I brought up to him the idea of structured time to process our cases, he really did not even understand what I was talking about.

"Process? What does that mean?"

"You know, talk through our cases."

"Oh well," he said, "you can do that at lunch or on your break."

We did not usually take breaks or eat lunch together. Lunch was either in the car or with coworkers, but we did not talk cases.

Overall, there was little understanding of what we needed as frontline workers or what it was like for us in the field, away from office cubicles. The expectation seemed to be that we should simply suck it up. We were all so busy, but ideally, there would have been a time set aside for discussion and feedback on cases. As it was, nobody really chatted. It was frustrating. Another day, another death.

Even so, I had a sense of pride in my job. I was doing work that many people did not want to do, and I was doing it very well, most of the time. That is all that mattered to my coworkers and myself. But it was very clear where the problem was—it was not with the patients; it was with the system.

It also became clear that I had a more difficult time with all this than most of my fellow social workers. I became close to one of my colleagues, but there was only one time when I really talked to her about a particularly challenging family. I became more emotional than I typically would be with a coworker. I was crying, and she was supportive at first.

"You know, you need to back off the involvement with the family—maybe we need to get somebody else in there," she suggested.

There was always a danger in getting too close to families, and sometimes that happened with me. This particular woman was leaving four young children behind. It does not get harder than that for me as a mother. I could not help but weep for that poor family.

My stress caught up with me, quite early on, during one of those quick-hit, ninety-minute meetings where we would quickly run through one patient after another in ways that were too superficial to be helpful. I was trying really hard to focus, but it became all too much. I am very comfortable hearing about emotional trauma, but the nonstop physical descriptions became overwhelming to me.

After that meeting, I went out to my car and lost it, crying. I sat in stunned silence, trying to absorb it all. I was used to grasping all the emotional, social, mental, facial, and even spiritual realities of my patients. But somehow, listening to the details—sometimes quite graphic—of the horrific physical conditions of thirty-two unique individual *people*, just being tossed about in a roomful of doctors, nurses, and social workers, so casually and bluntly, was just too much for me.

I was scared. I wondered, can I ever get used to this?

Chapter 3

All the Lonely People

Death by the numbers can be staggering.

I would be working with roughly fifteen to twenty-five hospice patients at any given time. About half of my caseload would die each month, invariably making room for more. That amounts to ten to fifteen deaths a month, maybe 125 a year. I did not go to all the funerals, perhaps a third of them. In three years, I met about three hundred people who would die well within the span of the same time period.

The official line at the hospice was that we did not "help people prepare for death," that we instead "helped them live life until the end of it." So untrue. It would have been cruel to not prepare someone for what was coming, as best we could.

After about eight months on the job, things became easier for me. I am not sure why. I suppose I got into the rhythm of working in the hospice environment and became somewhat hardened. I had been through a lot of death and dying by then, and so perhaps I had more confidence in my effectiveness. There is also this weird gallows humor that happens in hospices as a sort of coping mechanism—we would joke about a family that needed "slap therapy," for example.

Whatever the reason, I stopped crying all the time.

By then, I had also built up a couple of relationships with other staff members and had some degree of comfort there, but we still did not talk much about our cases. We just sort of ignored it, though we did talk about the agency and how dysfunctional it was. That was good for a laugh.

None of this is to imply that the work ever really got easier. Sometimes it would be a case of "hurry up and wait," and I got pretty good at that. If I was on call during the weekend, it was almost certain that I would get at least one call, so I might as well wait for it.

One morning at around 2:00 a.m., the phone rang—a rude awakening, even when you know it may be coming. The sister of one of my patients was very, very upset. Joan was going to die soon. The sister had thought she still had a couple of months to go, but things had taken a sudden downturn. She had finally grasped the true reality of her sister's impending death.

The woman on the phone was on the verge of hysterics. I remember asking her some specific questions, partly as a way to calm her down in the dark as I pulled on some semiprofessional clothes, trying not to disturb Ed or the sleeping pets. Putting the dogs out at 2:15 a.m. was the last thing I needed at this point. Time was of the essence.

The agency's rule was, I could not talk on the phone while I was driving. The problem was, Joan's death was very likely imminent, and she was a good twenty to twenty-five minutes away. At the same time, the sister seemed to need immediate support. It was a balancing act.

The sister did not know what to do and was scared to be alone. It is very hard to be the only one there when a loved one is dying. You do not want to leave them, even for a second. She sounded a little better by the time we hung up in the car. I quickly turned the key.

As I was frantically driving a late-night commute to a nearby town, I prayed Joan would survive until I arrived. It was so tempting to speed, but safely obeying speed limits was an agency rule. There is not much traffic at that hour, luckily.

When I finally rang the doorbell, a thirtysomething woman with messy short blond hair, a red nose, and sad, droopy eyes met me at the door. She nearly collapsed into my arms, but just as quickly stepped back, wiped her face with the back of her hand, and mumbled, "Sorry."

She grabbed my arm and pulled me into the living room, where a hospital bed was set up.

Thankfully, Joan was still alive, sleeping quietly, breathing slowly and unevenly.

I tried to calm down her sister and walk her through what was going on, explaining what the symptoms meant and what she could do in these final moments. I suggested that she sit and hold Joan's hand, talk to her, and try to keep her sister calm. I told her that even if a person is unresponsive, we still believe that they can hear us.

It was not long before Joan died quietly and peacefully as her sister lovingly held her hand. Another "good" death.

This was the kind of scene I would become accustomed to. A lot of people die at night. Perhaps it is easier to relax and at a time when we are used to falling asleep.

Some people even seemed to decide when to die. They simply let go. Many would die all by themselves. A family would hold vigil for a long period of time and then step out of the room for five minutes to have a conversation or go to the bathroom. When they got back, their loved one was gone. There were people who did not express a lot of emotion to their families during their moments of lucidity. Sometimes they would not even say "I love you" or "Goodbye."

One question came up a lot in my conversations with patients: "Whom are you having a hard time saying goodbye to?", I would ask. Sometimes the patients would want me to talk to their friends or family members or would at least want me to be there when they talked to them.

Other patients were mainly concerned with how their family was handling the situation. One was Monica, a twenty-seven-year-old nursing student with an inoperable brain tumor. She had short blond hair, large round blue eyes, and a slight build. She had fallen down and had a seizure outside her classroom at Stanford Medical School one day. There had been no history of medical problems.

Monica was about my daughter's age. Most of the young people I saw died of brain cancer. I did not do much life review with Monica or the other younger patients. Sadly, there was not a lot of life to review. Those cases took more of a toll on me than the older folks who had lived full lives. Fortunately, I never had children as patients, though I had colleagues who did.

Monica's family had brought her to a hospice wing in one of the local nursing homes. She had been given one to two weeks to live.

"Well, I guess this is it," she said when I first visited her.

In general, people were either pretty calm and settled about death, or they were pretty anxious and unfinished about it. This young woman was relatively accepting of her situation, lying on her bed, surrounded in this facility by people old enough to be her great-grandparents.

"This isn't what I wanted," she said with a sigh. "This isn't how I thought it would be, but here I am, and I want to help my family get through this."

Seeing her family in such emotional pain was very difficult for this young woman. She wanted me to help them more than help her. She was really brave. All you could do is just be with the family. There is not a lot you can say—and sometimes that *is* what you say.

This particular family did not want a lot of help. They wanted to be there for one another but did not really want assistance from an outsider, which I can certainly understand. The mother's tearstained face told the story of practically no sleep and countless hours at the computer and on the telephone to hospitals and specialists across the country looking for a miracle cure.

We did have one meeting with the whole family and the doctor, who went over what to expect in the final days and hours so they could "prepare," as much as they could. It was really tough.

I went to Monica's funeral and burial. Her mother collapsed as her daughter's body was lowered.

I ran into her a few years later and gently asked how she was doing.

"Thank you so much for asking. Well, I don't cry every day anymore," she said.

Another patient who had brain cancer, or glioblastoma, was Gene, thirty-eight. He was not a very pleasant man, especially to his wife, Cora. Gene ordered her around their small house, which was pretty messy most of the time. Cora had one bedroom devoted to sacks of clothes she would pick up at garage sales...a bit of a hoarder. As so often is the case with this behavior, the root cause was to be found in psychological pain. Cora would sometimes want me to meet her for a Coke at the fast-food restaurant where she worked. She said that it made her more comfortable to know that Gene could not hear her. During one of these meetings, Cora shared a painful history in their marriage of physical and verbal abuse. "Not bad enough to go to the hospital, or anything like that," she said, minimizing. But he would slap her or grab her arms and leave bruises and call her many bad names. She felt she had nowhere else to go. The little house was their only asset, and she planned on sticking around until Gene passed on so she could stay there. Cora shared that she had never spoken of this to anyone and that she felt relieved to be able to speak about it. When Gene did die, I was totally surprised to hear that the house where they had his memorial was filled to the brim with friends. Apparently, no one knew this bullying side of him, a secret closely guarded by both him and Cora. I referred her to the local safe house for support and counseling, but she declined both.

Unfortunately, not all families were emotionally available. I remember a woman with pancreatic cancer whose husband played golf every day, even though his wife was scared to be alone. That was difficult for me, but perhaps he was in denial or that was just his way of coping with it all. He seemed kind of nervous. Maybe he was uncomfortable being around her because he had no idea what to do. When I suggested we look at getting a volunteer to come in to stay with her, they both seemed relieved.

There was another case where a woman had been very, very close to her twelve-year-old grandson, but he refused to see her as soon as he found out she was dying. He just could not handle it. That really hurt his grandmother, until she began to understand.

After the funeral, I sought him out and told him his grandma had understood his difficulty and he should not feel badly about it. Another woman had a huge melanoma on her back. It was enormous and black. I could not help but think that if her husband had ever helped her undress, he would have caught the cancer sooner. It makes me cry for all those women out there whose husbands do not want to look at them anymore or whose wives are too embarrassed by their huge bellies to allow their husbands of twenty-five, thirty, or forty years to catch a glimpse of a strange-looking mole.

While apparent indifference was something I sometimes had to face, other families were downright hostile to the whole idea of hospice care.

Kim, a children's author, was very distraught about not being able to finish her last book. I could not help her with that, but she and I became quite close in a certain way, at least I thought so. When Kim was quite close to death, her son would not let me say goodbye. He was very "anti-hospice," for lack of a better word. He basically fired me from the case, and it hurt a lot to be dismissed like a servant.

Some family members did not seem to realize that a hospice social worker could provide them with practical information and resources that might be helpful, such as books to read, perhaps a support group, or just ironing out the details of the funeral. I was certainly willing to meet families on their own terms. But a few seemed to think I was just there to dig around in their psyche.

For some people, death just made no sense—at least not to them. Frank was forty-two and had an inoperable brain tumor. He was a biker who went with his girlfriend every year to the big motorcycle rally in Sturgis, South Dakota. They were sweet people. Frank could not believe he was going to die from this thing, which seemed like a big nothing to him. He had no real discomfort, except for the occasional headache. He really missed riding his bike.

For obvious reasons, older people, as well as their husbands, wives, and children, were much more accepting of death, and that was easier for me too. I always admired Betty, who was a resident at one of the nursing homes. She must have been eighty-five or so and was suffering from congestive heart failure.

Every day, Betty would look at the birds flying outside her window.

"Well, I wonder if that bird's gonna hit the window today," she would often remark. "Because you know, when that happens, it means somebody's gonna die today. And I wonder if it'll be me."

One of the saddest cases for me was a man, probably in his sixties, who was truly alone in life—and in death. Greg had melanoma that had spread throughout his body. Nobody ever came to visit him in the nursing home, and he had no friends there either. He was certainly a loner, but he did not want to be. He was not very easy to get along with, and evidently he never had been.

Still, Greg always looked forward to my visits because I would *really* talk to him. It was one of those situations where a hospice social worker can truly provide a crucial service. Unfortunately, I was not there when Greg passed away all by himself. In my experience, people die the way they lived, and that was certainly true in his case. That must be the saddest—to die lonely.

All Greg really had when he left the world was regret. He had a son who would never come to see him and a daughter he had no contact with at all. He told me that he had been a bad father. I did not meet the son, who lived locally, until after his father died. He came in for about ten minutes to see his dad's body. Then, he simply said, "I'm done," and then left the room with little emotion. It was quite unusual.

I was particularly touched by all the couples I worked with. At one point, I had three couples where the husband was caring for his wife. These gentlemen were all in their seventies or eighties, did not have children around, and took great care of their wives of fifty-plus years. The women all worried about what would happen to their husbands after they were gone and what would be left in their lives to do. One such man, Terry, planned on developing his woodworking interest, which he had let go of when his wife, Betty, got sick. Another, Tom, had decided to go to Arizona to live near his daughter...not too close, just within driving distance. The third, who believed his wife had mad cow disease dementia, had no plans. He didn't want any volunteer help at this point; he was quite capable of taking care of his beloved Sherrie himself.

I vividly recall another patient story with a situation of amazing tenderness. It was a long-married couple who were extremely close right until the very end. I cannot remember Matt's exact diagnosis, but he had central pain and a constant burning sensation throughout his entire body.

I met Matt the day before he died. His wife was Janet. It was snowing that day—big, soft, and beautiful. It must have been early spring. I walked up the four steps and rang the bell. The door opened, and a petite woman about my age with short brown hair and large brown eyes kindly swung the door open and said, "You must be Kathy." The living room was very warm—not the temperature, just inviting and comfortable. I felt right at home.

"Where would you like me to put my coat? It's a little wet."

She took it for me. She offered me coffee and wanted to just sit for a few minutes before I met her husband, and I thought that was a good idea. We spoke about the illness first, how long he had been diagnosed. Their kids—two daughters, twenty-seven and twenty-nine—both lived in town, one right there in the house, but they were not really there for Mom or Dad emotionally. That was very difficult for Janet.

"What's hardest about it now?" I asked.

After a long pause, she said, "I'll show you when we go upstairs, but I can't touch him anymore. It hurts too much. He just can't tolerate it. I can't even hold his hand or finger or put my foot against his toe. It's so bizarre and crazy and wrong. We've always had a very physical relationship, physical snuggling, and cuddling, holding hands. Now, nothing. It's like he's gone, except he's still here and they don't know for how long."

Janet did not know how much more she could take.

"It's torture. I adore him. I love him," she said.

Janet wanted to be "real" about her situation but did not have anyone to talk to, except me. I suggested she get a journal and start writing her feelings, hiding the journal from her daughters and even destroying it after she had written it, if she wanted to. I suggested she write it out as if she were talking to me. She liked that idea.

We went upstairs. It was a dark room with two twin beds, barely touching. Matt had very sad eyes, drugged eyes, heavy breathing, somewhat labored. I asked if he needed anything.

"No," he said. "Talk to my wife. She needs you, I think."

"Are you uncomfortable?"

"Yes," he said slowly.

I suggested the nurse could help with the pain, at least the physical pain.

"I want to say goodbye to my girls if they'll let me," he said. I promised to try to contact them.

He closed his eyes for some rest.

The next day, Matt passed away.

Just as they were about to remove the body, Janet fell into my arms.

"I didn't think it would be this hard," she said.

A short time later, we sat with her daughters, and they discussed the funeral arrangements; Janet was still clinging to my left hand. The young women were mostly quiet, occasionally wiping away a tear. Janet stood up. I followed her to the door.

"I hate to let you go," she said, "but I know you have other work to do."

As I left, walking down the front stairs, I felt a deep respect for Janet, for how she handled losing her love. I also felt good about the job I had done, basically by just showing up and being present. I guess that is what it is all about. She was very disappointed when I was not to be the promised grief counselor, but that was our policy. The Bereavement Team stepped in, and we disappeared.

As hard as that was, the most difficult death for me was Tanya, a twenty-four-year-old dancer with leukemia. She was delusional and highly anxious at the end. When I got there, she was lying in bed, her tiny body moving around pretty uncomfortably. Unfortunately, Tanya died before the nurse could get her calmed down. It was not a peaceful death. I only had a few hours with her. Tanya's parents were so traumatized to watch their young daughter suffer that way. Her mom fell against her husband with grief.

As I helped the funeral director move Tanya's body, I remember being shocked at how featherlight she was. My voice caught in my throat, and my eyes filled with tears as we lifted her off the bed. Tanya was so young. I could not help but think about my own daughters. I called them that night, just to say "Hi" and "I love you."

In a much different way, there was another case that was just as tough. In fact, it nearly ended my hospice career. From a purely professional standpoint, it was probably the worst.

It involved George, a dying father who, for whatever reason, did not want to see his daughter, Amy, who had flown in from Ohio for an eleventh-hour visit. My heart tugged for them both. Reconciling before death is beautiful when it can happen, but I also realized that it was not always possible.

I had no idea what the heck I was going to say to Amy—and before I could get my thoughts together, she walked in the front door.

"Where's my dad?" she asked frantically.

I calmly introduced myself and said I needed to speak with her for a minute. She understandably looked frustrated at this unknown person who wanted to talk to her.

"I'm sorry," I said, searching for my words. "I know you came all this way to see him, but George doesn't want to see you."

It was like a bomb dropped.

Amy took a moment to digest what I was saying.

"Of course, he'll see me. I'm his daughter," she said, clearly indignant and emotionally hurt. "What right do *you* have to keep me from him?"

"It's his request, not mine. It's his wishes we have to honor."

"But why?" Amy said, now more sad than angry.

I struggled to answer a fair and sensible question.

"I don't know, but he must have a reason."

That was the best I could muster, but it was not the right thing to say at all.

Amy flew off the handle.

"What right do you have to say that it's my fault?" she shouted. "He loves me. I know he does. You need to step aside."

I explained that I was not going to do that and that she needed to leave the house.

Finally, she left but warned she would be back.

I left the house too and sat in my car for a while. I realize now that I should have called my supervisor, but I was so used to handling things on my own. Frankly, the idea of asking for help did not even occur to me.

Unfortunately, that was not the end of the story. Several weeks later, I was told that Frank, the hospice's executive director, wanted to meet with me. Amy had written an angry letter of complaint. I went pale. I immediately felt scared and embarrassed. I was not permitted to see the letter before the meeting, which seemed unfair.

My supervisor, the RN on the case, another team leader, and Frank, the executive director, were all seated in this small room. As I walked in, I felt vulnerable. Frank explained that he had received two phone calls and now this letter from Amy, saying that I had—of my own volition—prevented her from seeing her dying father, that I was a horrible social worker, and that such an uncaring person should not be allowed on a hospice's staff. I should be fired immediately for incompetence, she demanded.

I felt completely humiliated and frightened for my job. Was I really incompetent and a bad social worker?

I tried to explain, but Frank interrupted, accusing me of mishandling the situation.

My supervisor tried to come to my defense.

"Let's give Kathy a chance to explain."

I described the events, the daughter's insistence, and the dad's need to have his wishes respected. I did not handle this the best way, I said, admitting that I am not the best at conflict. But I felt like my job was to protect the patient's rights, not the daughter's. I could have suggested Amy write him a note, but I did not think of that at the time.

I was asked to leave the meeting. I felt like crawling out.

To have my work questioned and criticized that way was painful. It felt like a personal attack. I met with my supervisor later that day. It was decided that Frank would try to smooth the waters. He would acknowledge Amy's right to be upset about not seeing her father and that, while I was following her father's wishes, I could have been more diplomatic.

I saw Frank later in the hallway.

"I'll be watching you," he said, ominously.

Was this a threat? I wasn't sure what to do with it. I felt alone and scared.

Chapter 4

Final Exit

Like a hospice worker who must eventually face her own mortality, I was also a longtime psychotherapist who clearly needed to spend some time on the other side of the counselor's desk. Although we had virtually no direct support as social workers, I did eventually take time to see a therapist, ironically through the agency's employee-assistance program.

"I think that would be a very difficult job," the counselor said.

That was about the extent of her observation. Not too helpful.

Eventually, I diagnosed myself with compassion fatigue. All caregivers are at risk for it because there is seldom enough support and the work is so emotionally exhausting. My own symptoms included chronic physical and emotional exhaustion, irritability, feelings of self-contempt, difficulty sleeping, weight gain, and not surprisingly, poor job satisfaction.

That would all come to a head in another ironic and emotional twist.

I found myself moving into the caregiver role when my aging parents experienced their own health crises. I had on-the-job training (for the technical aspects), but the emotional process was completely different for me. My sisters and I had to talk through our feelings often. My parents lived about a three-hour drive from our house. Conflicts with my work schedule were going to be inevitable, and I wasn't sure how to handle that.

My mother, who was about eighty-four, had always taken care of my father, who by now was eighty-eight and suffering from worsening dementia. But at this point, Mom was having health problems of her own. She needed back surgery and would require rehab after that.

At first, we hired caregivers for Dad, but that ran its course. It reached the breaking point one night when he went to the bathroom and locked the door. In his confusion, he began lighting matches and throwing them into the toilet, ostensibly trying to light a fire in what he thought was the gas stove. Thankfully, Dad had good aim, but it was all very scary. When he refused to unlock the door, the fire department had to be called. This was not what the caregivers had bargained for.

As an alternative to in-home care, we found an assisted-living facility where Dad could stay temporarily while Mom recovered, but it was very hard on him and us. It was time for the family to get more involved. I had a sister in town, but she was working full-time and had younger kids. She couldn't do it all. I felt that I wanted and needed to be there with my father.

One day, without taking much time to think about the professional consequences, I quickly packed a bag and headed for their town. I called the RN from the road. I felt panicky when I called her and said tearfully, "I'm checking out," and left in the middle of the day.

She had no idea what to do. The agency probably piled a few clients onto other social workers, but what was I supposed to do? My parents needed me. And I needed to be with them. I felt badly for my colleagues, but I did not feel like I had a choice. I was gone only a few days, but I would start driving back and forth every weekend.

The parallel processes of helping somebody from hospice get into an assisted-living facility and then helping my own father do the same thing was bizarre, to say the least. It was hard to separate it all out. I reached the point where I knew that I could not keep doing this.

I gave my notice to the hospice agency. This was hardly the thoughtful retirement I had planned, and unfortunately, my decision was not even the catharsis I might have hoped for. As it happened, the agency, was fine with my resignation, maybe too fine. In fact, they didn't really seem to care at all. The agency quickly replaced me. I think they hired an intern—not my idea of someone who could handle a *very* challenging job.

When I walked out the door six weeks later, there was no "Thank you" or "We'll miss you," much less a goodbye party. Instead, I was told I had not been a "good fit" anyway.

"I bet you'll be glad to get out of here," someone said.

It was all pretty disrespectful. The implication seemed to be that I could not handle it, that I was not strong enough for the job. Maybe some of that was true, but I hated to admit defeat.

Seeing so much pain, so many deaths, so many grieving faces and having to be the one comforting, shining light for all of them—every day and every night—was just too much. Why was it not too much for everyone else? Were my fellow social workers less involved than I was? Was that the little secret? Was I too emotional? Did I not have good boundaries?

Sadly, toward the end of my hospice tenure, I suspect that I might not have been "showing up" for the patients as much, in a meaningful sense. I had gotten pretty depressed, and I did not even really know it at the time. *Physician, heal thyself,* I thought.

About two weeks after leaving the job, I started having second thoughts about quitting. Go figure. I had been a failure for copping out, I began to think. But wait a minute. I am a strong person. I could go back and do this thing.

It was not to be, thankfully. A painful incident would bring clearer reflection.

During one of my weekends with my parents, I was taking Dad to visit Mom in the nursing home. We stopped to get some gas. When I got out of the car, I tripped on some gravel and fell hard. I managed to catch myself but broke *both elbows* in the process. There was no one around. It turned out that the gas station was closed. Fortunately, I had my cell phone in my pocket. I somehow managed to call 911. As I lay there helplessly, Dad had no idea what was going on.

But suddenly I did.

God was saying, "You're *not* going back to that job."

I was out of commission for six weeks—and it was a good thing in retrospect. There would be little opportunity for me to think "better" of my final decision. There was irony in not being able to care for myself after having cared for other people. With my broken elbows, I couldn't do anything. I couldn't do personal care. I couldn't get myself dressed; I couldn't even feed myself. Friends from Ed's work began to call and bring meals. No one from hospice ever did reach out.

Fortunately, as Dad began his sad, final decline, I was able to truly be there for Mom and my sisters. I strived to help them understand what was going on. It was a real blessing to share what I had learned with my family about the end of life. Although Dad was receiving his own hospice care by this time, I would once again understand the pain of my hospice families in a new, personal way.

Chapter 5

Reflections

I no longer have a fear of death.

That is quite a change for me. I was once terrified by the very thought of dying. This healthy evolution in my outlook did not come in spite of my difficult hospice work, but largely because of it. Although I witnessed great sadness, I also saw moments of beautiful peace.

Still, there is more to the story.

I suppose I had always believed in God, but I really had no real idea what that meant. Maybe I was a Christian, but a pretty basic one. I did not know if there was really a heaven. Honestly, I did not even think about it too much until hospice work slowly changed my spiritual perspective.

As a function of my job, I would talk a lot about religion with my clients—what they believed and how that affected their feelings about death. Those discussions eventually got me thinking more about my own path, or my lack of a discernible one. Talking about existential questions of life after death became part of my job description and, eventually, a part of my life.

One day, after a particularly harrowing situation, I remember being completely exhausted. I was at my desk, right next to Nicky, one of our chaplains. She happened to be a Catholic. She always seemed upbeat and peaceful inside. I leaned over and asked her, with a shaky voice, "How do you do it? I'm not handling this job very well."

After a long pause, she answered.

"I go to the foot of the cross," she said.

This was way too graphic for me. "I can't do that," I said.

"That's not where you are?" she asked.

I just shook my head.

About three years after leaving my job, my husband, Ed, and I started looking around for new church to go to, though I did not think of this search as having much to do with my hospice work at the time. Ed had been raised Catholic, and I had been brought up in a very liberal, socially minded church. We had hoped to find something that was more or less a compromise between the two. I had a pretty big dislike of Catholicism in those days, so I did not think that would be an option, even though at the time I really did not know very much about the religion, to be honest.

Then one day, something very strange and unexpected happened. We had gone to get coffee at Starbucks, just killing time before a prospective church service. Almost as soon as I sat down, I burst into tears and said to my husband, "I need to go to a Catholic church." It was a total mystery. My realization seemed to come out of nowhere.

I am sure Ed was surprised by my unexpected "revelation," but he was very supportive. First time we went to a Catholic church, I immediately felt God's presence. I had finally come home.

Still, sometimes things in life happen in a weird and awkward order. If I had already been a Catholic when I worked for the hospice, would my job have been easier, and would I have been far less stressed? I think, yes, I might have been a better social worker if I had been a Catholic at the time.

There is a certain consolation that happens in Catholicism that I had never experienced before. As a comforting result, I have tremendous acceptance of life and death. I know where to go now when I am anxious, fearful, or sad. I am at peace with the things that once caused me enormous stress. Having said that, I do not think it was a "mistake" that I took that job when I did. I believe God must have wanted me there. Life is not always easy—and neither is death. I had learned some valuable lessons.

It does not surprise me that the hospice patients I met who held a spiritual belief of some sort had an easier transition. Those patients would talk about death with a sense of peace and were often eager to see others they had lost in life or to be in heaven or with God. I remember one woman who, as she died, held her arms up in the air, her eyes wide open, as if she were reaching for something or someone.

I remember, as I sat with another woman, a retired teacher who had slowly lost her sight to macular degeneration; she told me she had just seen—quite literally—one of her former principals, a man who had died some years earlier, arrive at the door of her room and tell her he was ready for her to come. She was so happy to see him. She died a few days later.

Of course, none of us know how we will respond when the time comes. But I can say that the sum of my experiences—both professional and spiritual—is that I am entirely conscious and accepting of what one day will be my inevitable exit from this world. One cannot count on the ability to plan it all out, of course, but my fantasy is that my family would be there at the end, just to enjoy being with me and with one another. I would much rather be the person who has a chance to say goodbye than someone who goes out unexpectedly. I like closure. A friend and I have agreed to destroy each other's journals.

One thing is certain. If I were to wind up in hospice care, I would have an interesting conversation with my social worker. I also know I would be one of *those* patients who would be more prone to choose comfort over alertness. I would do all I could to get rid of an awful pain. I have seen way too much of it.

Working for hospice was a very humbling experience for me. I walked in the door thinking I knew a lot, but I finally learned that I could not do it all on my own. I was good at certain aspects of my job, but not all of them. I needed other people and God, but I had too much pride to admit it.

I had been in private practice for a long time and was pretty independent when I walked into the hospice building for the first time—and that is not necessarily a good way to be. As I realized over time, it is not really important how smart or talented you are. What is important in hospice work is to be present with people and to be authentic.

It may be ironic that I found a lot of strength in my work overall, even though I felt defeated at the end. What emerged was a better and stronger person.

A bright side of it all is that hospice work, for all its faults and my own, has helped change the way I live—and certainly the way that I will one day die, if it's from a lengthy illness. I will choose pain control over awareness at the end. I am now grateful every single day, particularly for my marriage. Ed and I both are—and we are not afraid to express that. We do not just assume that the other person knows how we feel. In fact, I have become overtly thankful, in general, with my friends, my daughters, and my grandkids. The present moment is all we have.

Another gift I gained from my work was the skill to listen and to truly be there for people in any situation. If I were to die tomorrow, I believe that everything important has been said to those I love and respect. Thankfully, I do not believe I will have those kinds of regrets in life or death. Of course, I will miss people. It will be hard to say goodbye to them. But I am not afraid of doing it.

Like countless meaningful things in life, the whole of hospice was overwhelming: so many patients and deaths, extreme pain and so many illnesses, a multitude of families distressed emotionally, sometimes suffering silently. Even with all these very difficult situations, there were blessings and gifts: I learned that people are extraordinarily strong, patients and families. I was blessed to witness so many beautiful, soft, gentle passings. I became extremely good at listening and reading nonverbal cues. I gained an enormous respect for nurses and the other disciplines at hospice and the many volunteers who gave so generously of their time.

I did not deal with my own anguish at the time. I stuffed my feelings deep inside myself. The patients were suffering physically from pain and from the emotional loss of their own life and the loss of everything in their lives—their friends, families, pets, mental faculties, or bodily functions. Meanwhile, their families were suffering the loss of their dear loved one, the connection to their life, their sense of life in their family circle. Some of them chose to face the loss head-on and be present. Others couldn't.

Toward the end of my work there, I was dealing with personal loss too. My parents' health was declining. Dad's dementia was on a downward spiral. It was a blessing to share what I had learned in hospice with my family. Unlike my sisters, I was already accustomed to watching the sad decline of a once-vibrant soul. A strange kind of luck, I guess, but I had a certain acceptance as my parents neared their end.

One night, my family played cards.

The next day, I said, "You did really well last night, Dad."

"Did we play cards last night?"

"Yeah, and you did great."

He laughed, seeing the irony as his memory failed him.

The most touching death I ever witnessed on the job was one in which everyone in the large family was crowded around the bed, with a priest, holding hands and praying and giving their dying father permission to go. He died peacefully.

That really set the scene for what I want. When my father was actively dying, we sisters gathered in my parents' room at the nursing home. Dad was resting comfortably, curled up in the bed. We told stories and sang some of his favorite songs, gently saying goodbye, each in our own way. When he died, I was not there, sadly. I had gone to rest after having been awake all night. I would have liked to have been there, but perhaps this is the way Dad wanted it, somehow protecting the youngest.

Mom was in a nursing home when she passed on. I really wanted to be there, especially since I had not been present for Dad. When my sister left to take a nap in another wing, I stayed. As the youngest child, I was particularly close to Mom. I knew she was close to death. All of us had already had a chance to say goodbye to her several times, but this time I knew it was real.

I knew the time was very near, and I tried to reach my sisters. One said she didn't want to be there. Another couldn't get there soon enough, and my other sister was resting. I was alone with Mom when the end came. It was just an amazing experience to be the family member there, instead of the social worker, and to be truly close to her in that moment. I was able to give her permission to go because I could see that she was deliberately hanging on by a thread.

"I know you're ready," I said tearfully. "You're ninety-one, you're tired of this, and we're all going to be okay."

Mom closed her eyes and died a short time later.

I was really, really comfortable in that setting.

Yes, by then, I had traveled a crooked road with lots of side trips and spent lots of hours in therapy, many days philosophizing as I strived to heal wounds and get clarity about who I was, what I believed, and where I was going. I am not finished yet, of course. Today is another day.

As I said, I am not afraid of death. But just as important, I am not afraid of life.

About the Author

Katherine A. Cullen holds a master's degree in social work and is a retired licensed clinical social worker. While most of her more than thirty-year career was spent in private practice counseling adults, couples, and families, she also worked in several social service agencies.

Kathy started her career working in mental health centers doing therapy. She also worked with pregnant teens as they decided whether or not to parent. She has also worked in a juvenile detention center, two psychiatric hospitals, an agency providing services to those people with very low incomes, and at a safe house for battered women. She has taught several courses at a university in the social work department.

She is now retired and lives in Colorado with her husband, near their children and grandchildren.

CPSIA information can be obtained
at www.ICGtesting.com
Printed in the USA
LVHW110310110621
689683LV00025B/373

9 781646 544363